FLOWER AND GARDEN

WOMEN AND FLORAL THEMES DESIGNS

COLORING BOOK FOR ADULTS

I0407942

Copyright: Published in the United States

Published 2017

All rights reserved.

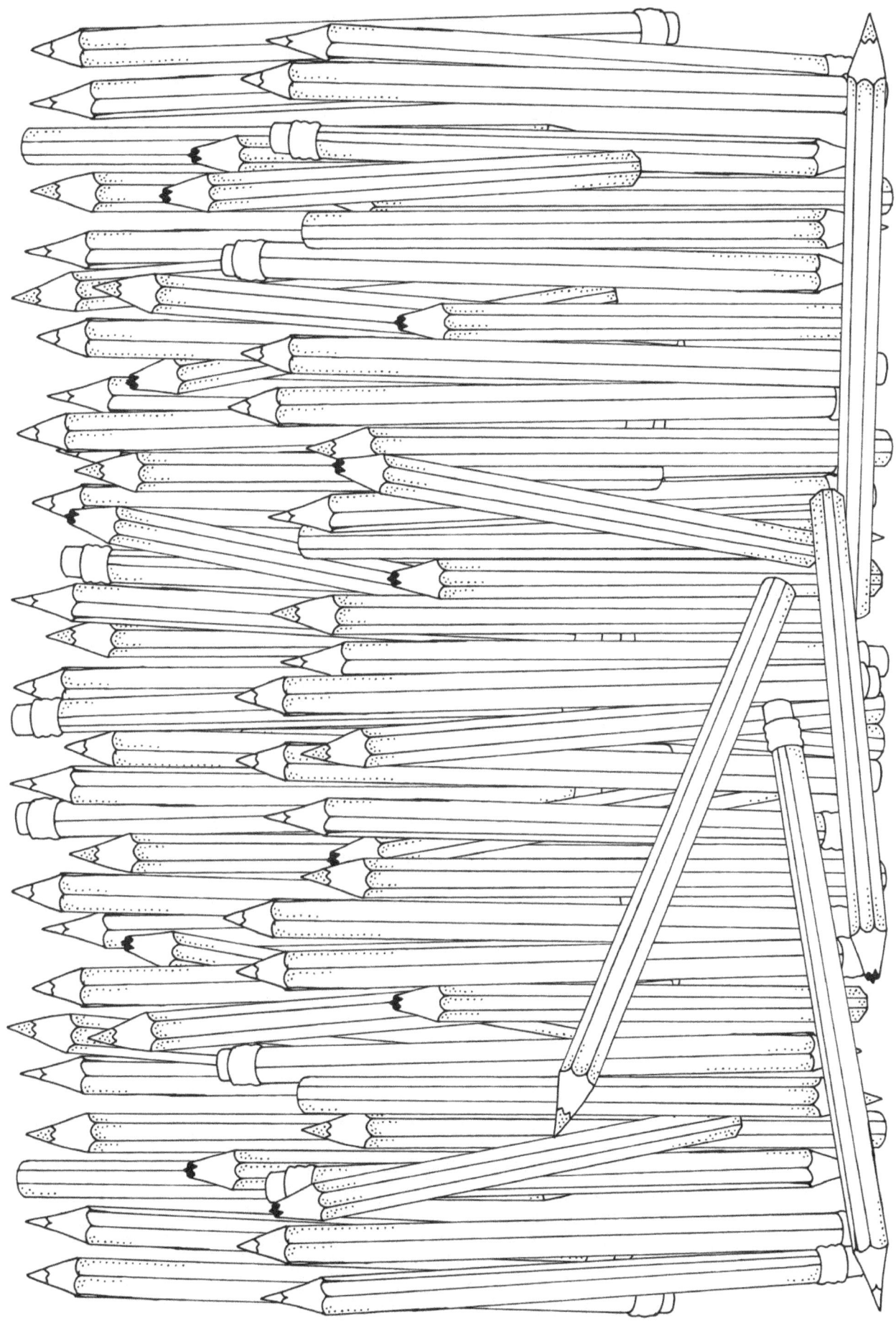

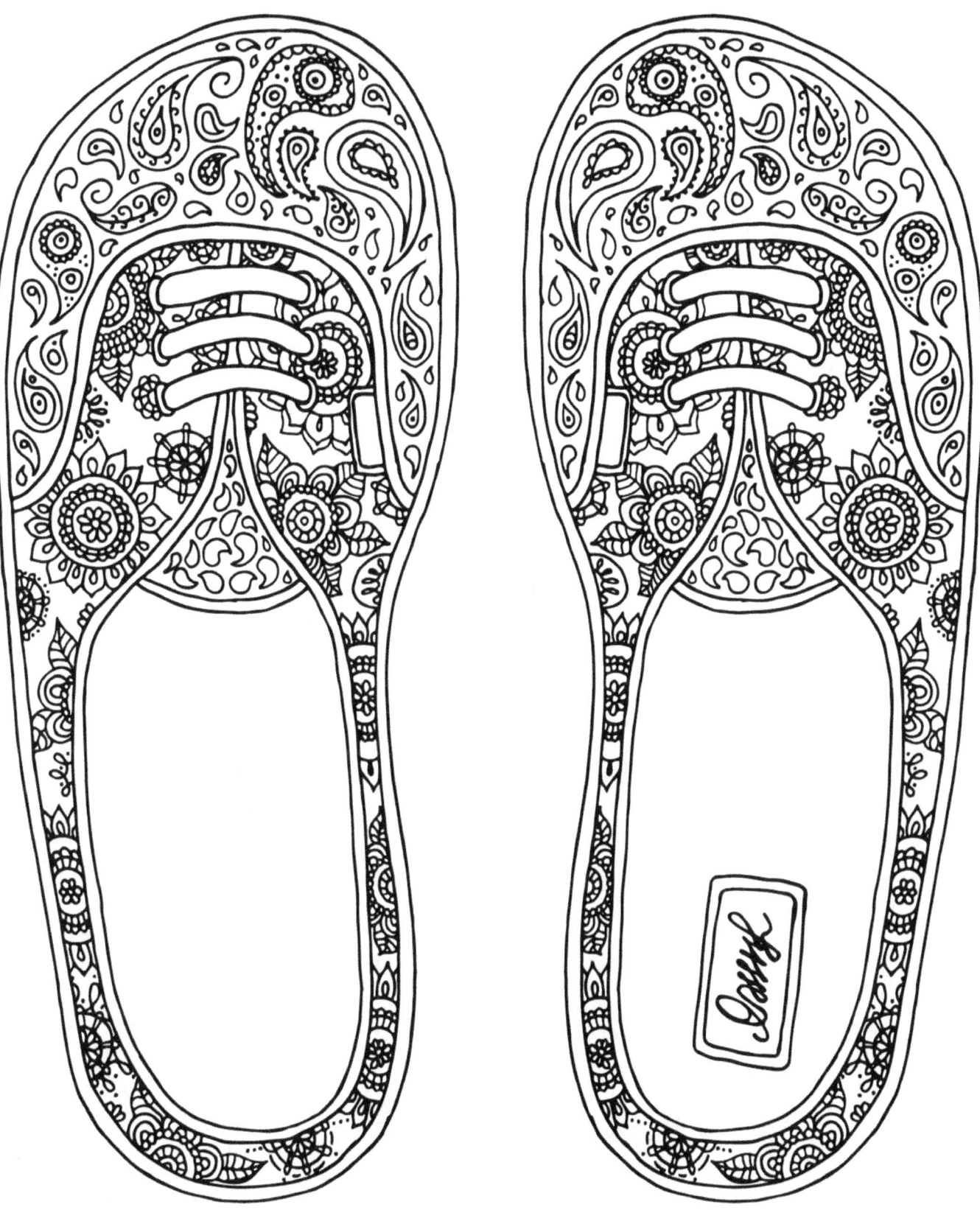

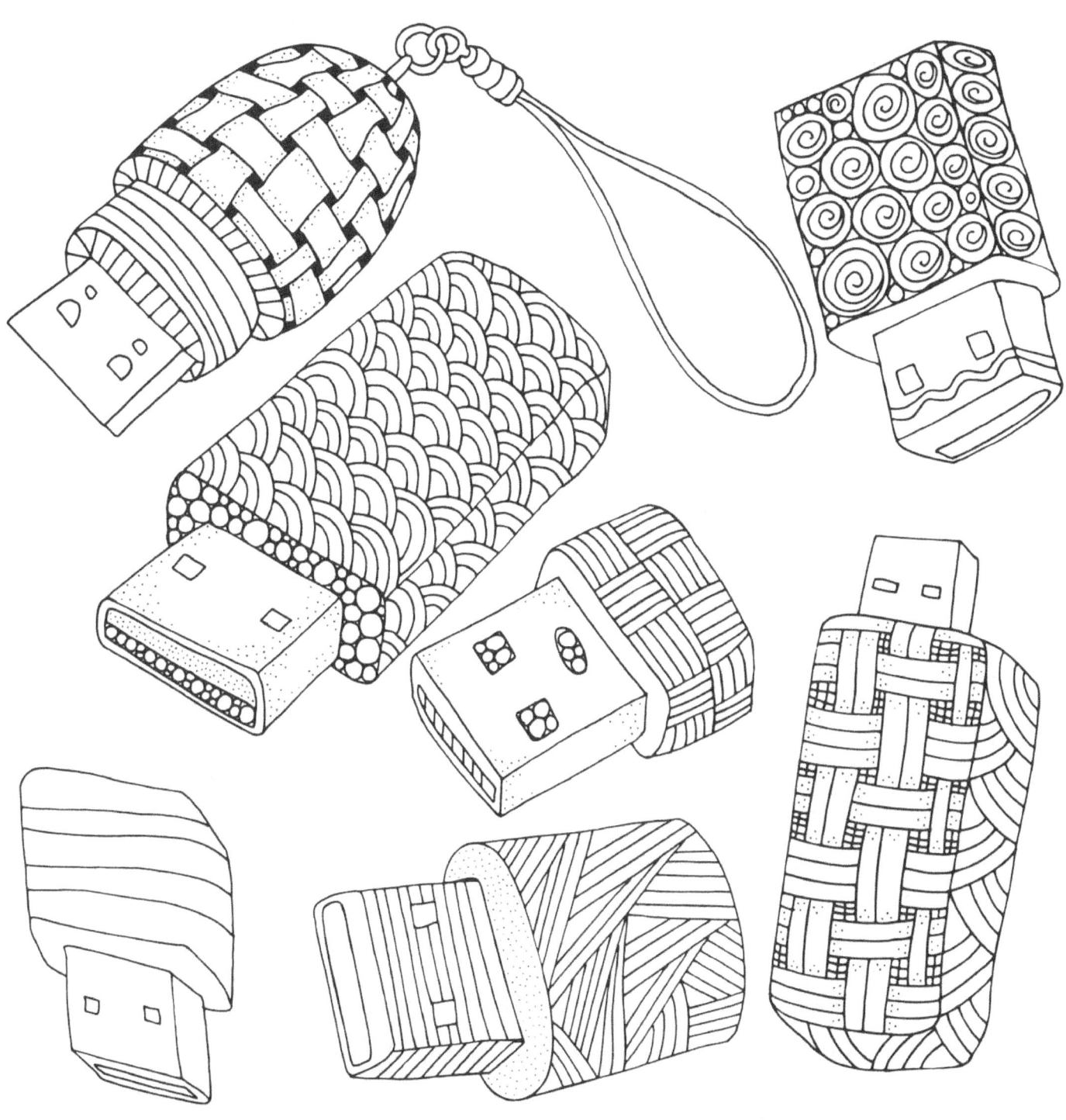

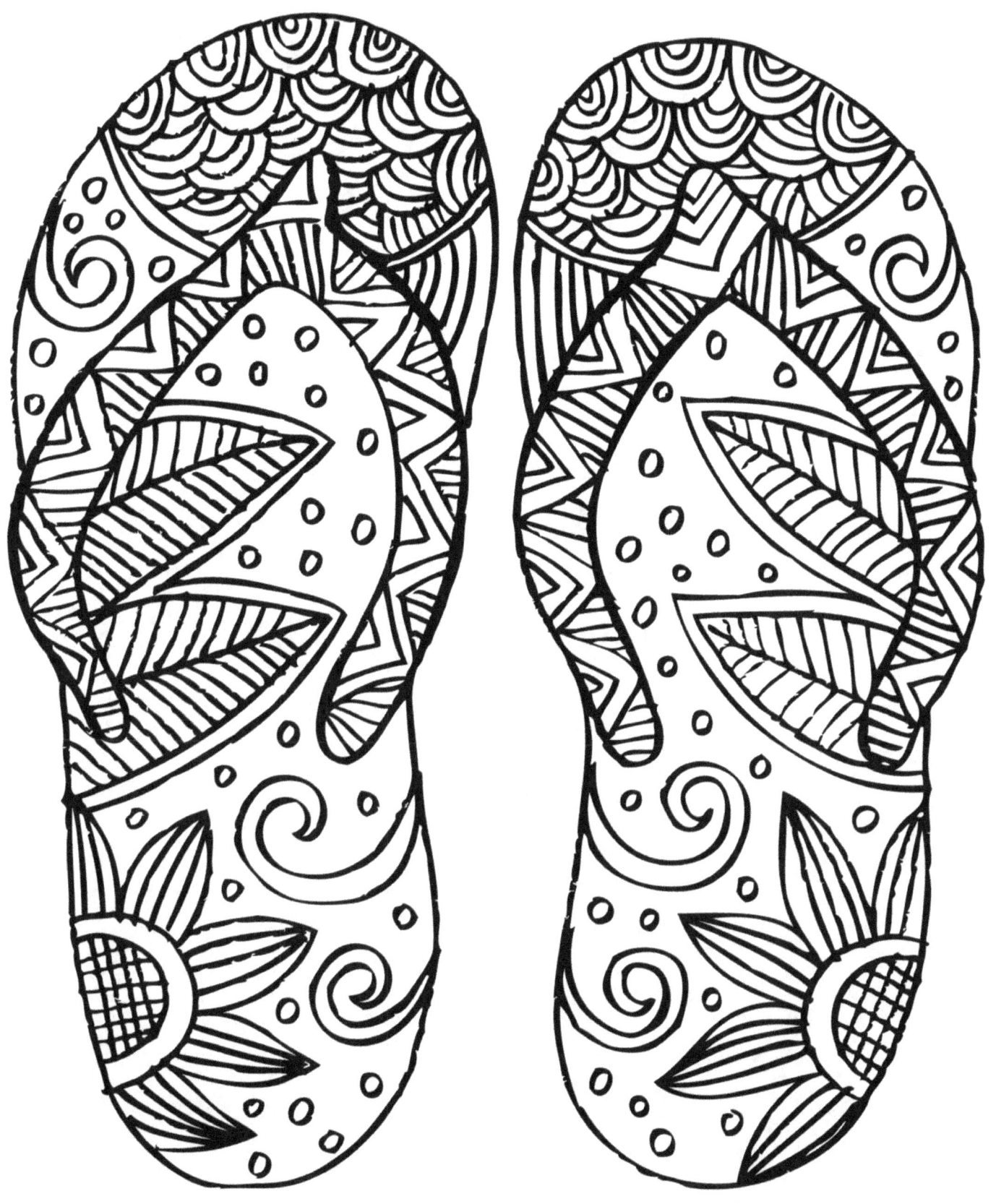

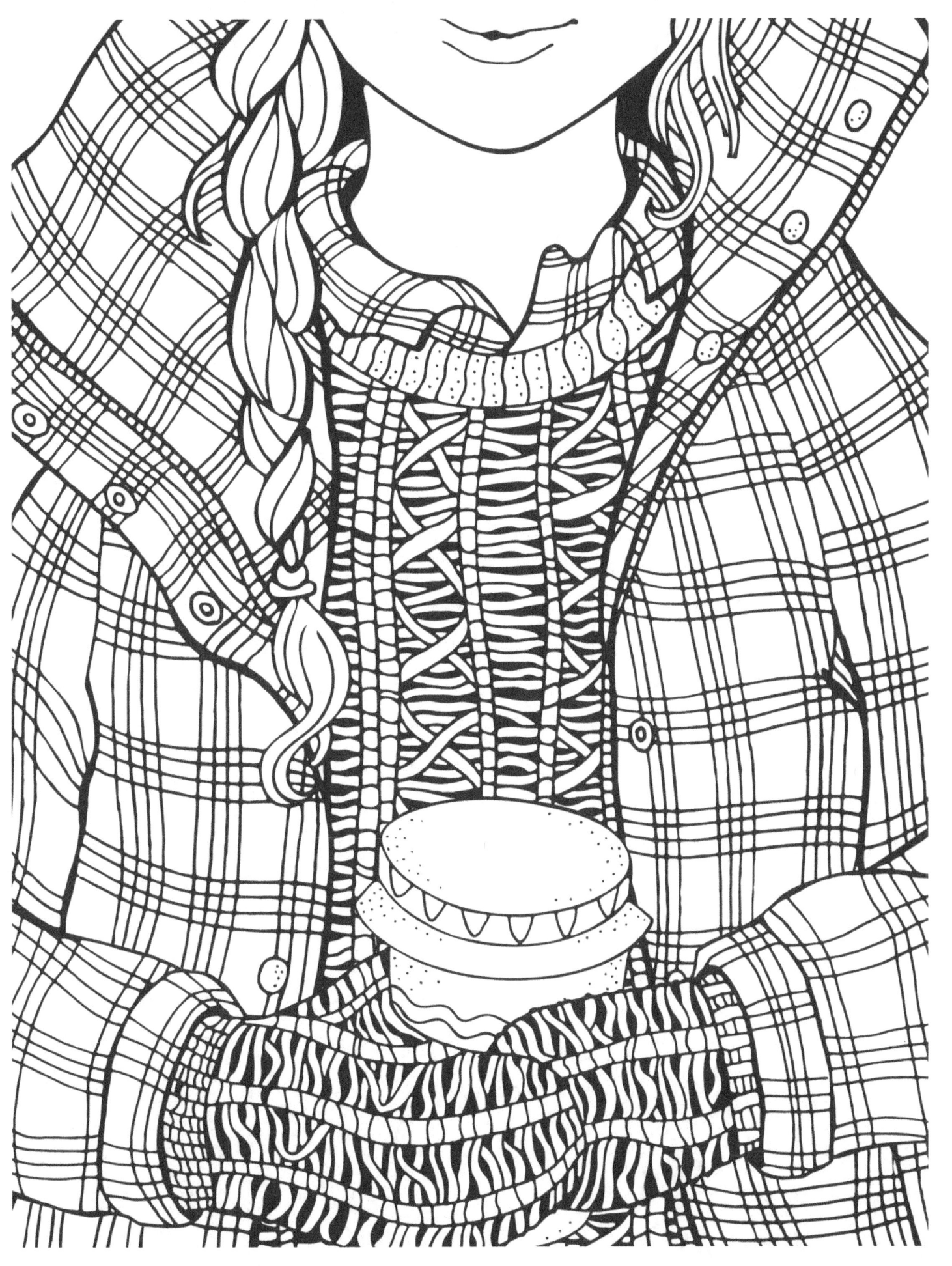

www.ingramcontent.com/pod-product-compliance
Lightning Source LLC
Chambersburg PA
CBHW081601280526
45788CB00011B/3534